THE GREAT SAN FRANCISCO EARTHQUAKE AND FIRE

"Taken from Accounts
of the Most Appalling Disaster
of Modern Times
by James Russel Wilson
the Well-known Author"

A Cycle of Found Poems
Based on Wilson's Memorial Volume
San Francisco's Horror of Earthquake and Fire
(Philadelphia 1906)

John Robert Colombo

THE GREAT SAN FRANCISCO EARTHQUAKE AND FIRE

Fiddlehead Poetry Books

for George Jonas

The Great San Francisco Earthquake and Fire was broadcast by the CBC on " Anthology," Saturday, December 26, 1970.

One thousand copies of John Robert Colombo's *The Great San Francisco Earthquake and Fire* have been printed by Fred Cogswell (Fiddlehead Poetry Books), Fredericton, N.B., Canada, 1971.

Printed in England. Cover design by David Shaw.

IBSN-0-919196-51-9

The world exists to end in a book.
— Stéphane Mallarmé

If it has been lived or thought it
will one day become literature.
— Emile Zola

But there was no panic.
The people were calm, stunned.
They did not seem to realize
the extent of the calamity.
They heard that the city
was being destroyed;
they told each other
in the most natural tone
that their residences were destroyed
by the flames, but there
was no hysteria,
no outcry,
no criticism.

But I was just stunned.
I stood there in the street
with debris falling about me.
It seemed the natural thing
for the tops of buildings
to careen over
and for fronts to fall out.
I do not even recall
that the women screamed.

San Francisco is apparently gone.
To the west, across the bay,
there is nothing but a great cloud of smoke,
shot with streams of fire,
and shaken now and then with the dynamite explosions
by which they are trying vainly to check it.
The fire is now everywhere.

Men and women were all about us.
We looked at each other and talked;
even tried lamely to joke.
But every few minutes
a convulsive quiver
swept through the city.
The others seemed to be shivering.
I noticed that the eyes of the men and women
were rolling restlessly.
Their tones were pitched high.
It seemed to grate on my nerves.
Then I fell to wondering
whether I was talking shrilly, too.

The situation was summed up in a telegram
sent Thursday morning by General Funston
to the War Department at Washington.
It read as follows: "It could not be worse."

And all this time,
and clear up until noon,
the earth was shaking
with little tremors,
many of which brought down
walls and chimneys.
At each of these
the rescuers,
even the firemen,
would stop for a moment
paralyzed.

The earthquake, however,
had broken
most of the water mains,
and the men were without water
to battle with the fire.
Whatever water was obtained
to fight the flames in the harbor front
and in the factory districts
was pumped from the bay.
This compelled dynamiting
as the only possible method
of saving any of the city.

During the day
a blast could be heard
in any section
at intervals of only
a few minutes,
and buildings
not destroyed by fire
were blown to atoms.

It was resolved to make a last stand
on the broad thoroughfare, Van Ness Avenue.
A line of residences a mile and a half long
was marked for sacrifice,
in hope that the flames might not be able
to leap the space left by the ruins
and the 100 feet of the street.
But almost before execution of the plan was begun
the fire was across the avenue
and the final act of San Francisco's annihilation
was entered upon.

"No more dynamite! No more dynamite! "
a fireman ran shrieking up Ellis Street
past the doomed Flood Building
at 2 o'clock Friday morning,
and as he ran tears sprang from his
smoke-smirched eyes. "No more dynamite! "
moaned the crowd that stood in the glare
of approaching flames.
"No more dynamite and we are lost! "

All through the day
it was much like night
on account of the smoke.

The day of awful disaster
was followed by a night of terror —
a black night of terror —
for the city was in darkness,
save where the crushed and ruined
heart of the city
flared red with fire.

Not alone were the parks the places of refuge.
Every large vacant lot in the safe zones
had been pre-empted, and even the cemeteries
were crowded. A well-known young woman
of social position, when asked where she had
passed the night, replied, "On a grave."

A son of T. P. Riordan,
a real estate dealer,
was shot and instantly killed
a few feet from his residence.
Young Riordan was on his way home
and had a bottle of whiskey
in his coat pocket.
The soldier on duty
ordered him to stop
and throw the whiskey away,
and when Riordan refused
the soldier immediately shot him dead.

Not less than fifty men paid with their lives
the penalty of either their cupidity or their indiscretion.
One was shot by a guard for washing his hands in drinking water,
a commodity that was being husbanded as sacredly
as though it were molten gold. Another, who was a bank clerk,
was shot by a soldier while searching after nightfall
amid the ruins of the bank in which he had been employed.

One man, a foreigner,
not understanding English,
started to walk away
when a militiaman
ordered him to chop some wood.
Without more ado,
the guard raised his rifle
and fired,
injuring the other fatally.
Such cases as these
were numerous.
All but the regulars
were wrought up
to a high pitch of excitement
and shot where milder orders
would have sufficed.

One peculiar thing
is that almost everyone
thought that the end of the world
was at hand.
Native sons of San Francisco
had experienced earthquakes before.
This was something new.
It was not an earthquake.
It was something worse.
They had no communication
with the outside world.
Naturally, they imagined
that the disturbances
which were taking place in 'Frisco
were being repeated
all over the country.
This belief was universal.

"I met ex-Mayor Phelan on the street yesterday
and he asked me to get some sort of a notice given out
to the public that their losses would be paid.
I do not believe that this is the proper thing,
and I told him so. The companies I represent
will pay what they are liable for and no more,
and it is better for those whose spirits are drooping
to allow them to droop rather than to buoy them up
with false hopes." From the remark made
there was no doubt that the companies
would draw a fine distinction
between the loss by earthquake and that by fire,
and would only pay for that which was actually burned.

The only institution on Market Street able to do business
was, according to a reliable business man,
the Market Street Bank, at Seventh and Market Streets.
Although the upper part of this building
and every building near it was wiped out,
the space occupied by the bank was undamaged.
A sign posted in the window stated that the bank
would be open for business as soon as it was considered safe.

On the step of one bank,
with the fire only a block away,
I see a man wringing his hands
and crying aloud:
"Will he never come?
Will he never come with the combination?
My God, why doesn't he come?"

Governor Pardee
announced
that he would continue
to proclaim
legal holidays
from day to day
as long as the
financial condition
of the State
was unsettled.

Heroic deeds,
many of which
will never be known
to the world,
were done hourly.

Governor Pardee, of California,
announced his belief
that the salvation of the city
was being worked out successfully,
and that a finer metropolis
would be reared over the ruins.

Weddings in great number
resulted from the disaster.
Women, driven out of their homes
and left destitute,
appealed to the men to whom
they were engaged,
and immediately marriages were effected.

"I don't live anywhere,"
was the answer given in many cases
when the applicant for a license
was asked where his residence is.
"I used to live in San Francisco."

A crowd of soldiers was sent
to the Flood and Huntington mansions and Hopkins Institute
to rescue the paintings.
From the Huntington home and the Flood mansion
canvases were cut from the framework with knives.
The collections in the three buildings
were valued in the hundreds of thousands.
Few were saved from the ravages of the fire.

See the people flee!
Here is a woman,
a parrot in one hand,
a milliner's creation
in the other,
followed by her husband,
with a tin teapot
and a woman's silk dress.
He would do better
to carry a blanket.
He will need it.

Food is at famine prices.
Oranges, two for 25 cents.
A San Mateo County milkman
comes along. He wants
$5 per can for his milk.
A member of the crowd
offers him a dollar per can.
He refuses, and in a minute
the crowd empties his wagon,
carrying off the cans,
and he gets not a penny.
Served him right.

I went to a grocery without a front
and bought a few supplies —
things that would make a cold lunch.
The grocer did not even overcharge me.
He was particular
to give me the right change.

I had a small leather grip with me
and I stuffed it full of pies
which I bought in a little restaurant.
They were the only food in sight.
Later I purchased several bottles of ginger beer,
so while hundreds about us
were suffering in the next twenty-four hours
for want of food and drink,
we had plenty of both.
I never knew pie was so wholesome.

On Thursday morning
we managed to get a conveyance
at enormous cost,
and spent the entire day
in getting to the Palace.
We paid a dollar apiece for eggs
and a dollar for a loaf of bread.
On these and a little ham
we had to be satisfied.
We reached Oakland on a ferryboat,
and are now trying to get back
to Los Angeles.

The freaks of the earthquake
were marvelous.
Some of the streets were twisted,
others showed the effects
of the earth waves
and were a mass of little depressions
and undulations.

Not until the earthquake
shook the rickety houses
to the earth
to be destroyed by fire
did the authorities of San Francisco
realize what manner of place
was the much-advertised Chinatown,
the Mecca of all tourists in California,
the post in which 25,000 Chinese
lived like so many prairie dogs.

For years I have been trying
to reach the tunnels
which I knew to exist
under this Chinese city.
What goes on down there
one can only conjecture,
but it is a thousand times worse
than the sins and vices
which are practiced
by these Mongolians in the streets
and gambling houses you can see
from this corner.
Girls in the bloom of youth
are smuggled over the Canadian border,
brought here in the night,
and confined in dungeons,
perhaps never to look upon
the light of the sun again,
although they may live for years.

The Chinese came out of their
underground burrows like rats
and tumbled into the square,
beating such gongs and playing
such noisy instruments
as they had snatched up.
They were met
on the other side
by the refugees
of the Italian quarter.
The panic became a madness.
At least two Chinamen
were taken to the morgue
dead of knife wounds,
given for no other reason,
it seems,
than the madness of panic.

No wonder the Chinese,
from the traditions of centuries,
have built up a belief
in a huge dragon,
the earth's dragon,
that sleeps underground.
To this day the Empress of China
refuses permission to dig mines,
and even to build railroads,
for fear of irritating
the earth's dragon.
This superstition of an old nation
is born of the rumbling,
crashing and deaths
that frightened the Chinese
in earthquakes centuries ago.

From their doors were issued
a motley throng of Chinamen,
clad only in their queerly figured pajamas,
fighting among themselves in fear
that one might find a better
means of escape than the other.
Here and there in the crowd,
growing larger and more turbulent every moment,
was a small group of painted white women,
what we in 'Frisco call "the white Chinese."
Strange to say, such a group was always
accompanied by a mighty Chinese guard,
who hewed a way through the throng
for the women in his charge.
I saw one of the women go mad from fear,
striking out at her own protectors,
and then escape from their custody.

While I was walking down the streets
I saw man after man shot down by the troops.
Most of these were ghouls.
One man made the trooper believe
that one of the dead bodies
lying on a pile of rocks
was his mother, and he was permitted
to go up to the body.
Apparently overcome by grief,
he threw himself across the corpse.
In another instant the soldiers discovered
that he was chewing the diamond earrings
from the ears of the dead woman.
"Here is where you get what is coming to you,"
said one of the soldiers,
and with that he put a bullet through the ghoul.
The diamonds were found in the man's mouth afterward.

A. W. Hussey came to the station
at the Hall of Justice
and told how, at the direction of a policeman
whom he did not know,
but whose star number he gave as 615,
he had cut the arteries in the wrists
of a man pinioned under timbers
at the St. Catherine Hotel.
According to the statement made by Hussey,
the man was begging to be killed,
and the policeman shot at him,
but his aim was defective
and the bullet went wide of the mark.
The officer then handed Hussey a knife,
with instructions to cut the veins
in the suffering man's wrists,
and Hussey obeyed orders.
Chief of Police Dinan directed
that Hussey be locked up.
There was no opportunity to investigate his story,
but the police believed that the awful calamity
rendered him insane,
and that the incident reported to them
had no existence excepting in his imagination.

We went to Agnews, where we had a friend,
and found the asylum in ruins
and 200 demented creatures buried there.
It was a sight to transfix one with horror
to see scores of mad men and women
strapped to trees all over the grounds,
crying, shrieking and cursing.
Ordinarily troublesome in their way,
the excitement of the falling building
made them mad indeed,
and their uncanny looks and fiery eyes
were terrible to behold.
Nothing could be done for them,
as there was no place to put them,
and every sane man, woman and child available
was digging to release
the other unfortunates buried in the ruins.
Oh, such cries as came seemingly
out of the bowels of the earth!
"The devils have got me; let me out!"
"I am the king; you cannot kill me!"
"I want my supper. I want my dinner!"
Just as the vagary seized them
they called out their disorganized thoughts
before they even guessed their true condition.

Near the Japanese tea garden
I heard a child crying,
and presently found a tiny child
tied to a tree.
A soldier sentry passing
told me that the child's mother
had been taken away by the doctors,
who said she had smallpox.
The father had gone away
to procure food,
and the mother had caused the doctor
to tie her child to the tree
so that its father might find it
when he returned,
and to the little one's dress
was pinned a note
informing the father
what had become of the mother.

From the southern section of the city —
from the ramshackle houses where the carnage was frightful —
half-clad children and women and men
came running, crying shrilly in their terror.
The foreheads of some of them showed red wounds.
Some fell in dead swoons. Children
made motherless in the night
clung to strange women for protection.

I climbed to the top of Strawberry Hill,
in Golden Gate Park,
and saw a woman, half naked,
almost starving, her hair disheveled
and an unnatural lustre in her eyes,
her gaze fixed upon the waters in the distance,
and her voice repeating over and over again:
"Here I am, my pretties; come here,
come here." I took her by the hand
and led her down to the grass at the foot of the hill.
A man — her husband — received her from me
and wept as he said: "She is calling
our three little children.
She thinks the sound of the ocean waves
is the voices of our lost darlings."

Last night a soldier seized me
by the arm and cried:
"If you are a woman with a woman's heart,
go in there and do whatever you can."
"In there" meant behind a barricade of bush,
covered with a blanket,
that had been hastily thrown together
to form a rude shelter.
I went in and saw one of my own sex
lying on the bare grass naked,
her clothing, torn to shreds,
scattered over the green beside her.
She was moaning pitifully,
and it needed no words to tell a woman
what the matter was. He ran off
and soon two sympathetic ladies
hastened into the shelter.
In an hour my escort returned
with a young medical student.
Under the last ministrations we could find,
a new life was ushered into this hell,
which, a few hours ago, was the fairest among cities.

Over in a corner of the plaza
a band of men and women were praying,
and one fanatic,
driven crazy by horror,
was crying out at the top of his voice:
"The Lord sent it, the Lord! "

A man, running half naked,
tearing at his clothes and crying,
"The end of all things has come! "
was caught by the soldiers
and placed under arrest.

"When the fire caught the Windsor Hotel,
at Fifty and Market," said Mr. Fast,
"there were three men on the roof,
and it was impossible to get them down.
Rather than see the crazed men
fall in with the roof
and be roasted alive
the military officer directed his men
to shoot them, which they did
in the presence of 5,000 people."

One of the gruesome scenes
that followed the fire
was that witnessed
on Telegraph and Russian Hills
and along the entire
north beach front of the city,
when scores of half-starved dogs
were found eating human bodies.

A theatrical man comes running along
telling how the Grand Opera House
has fallen in and is on fire
with all Conreid's grand opera settings
and the singers' beautiful things
going up in smoke. He laughs idiotically,
poor chap, and says:
"Sudden close of the opera season,
isn't it?"

"The last I saw of poor, speechless Caruso
was when he was driven off on top
of a loaded truck toward Golden Gate Park.
You see, the earthquake had a terrible effect on him,
considering the fact that he had just promised
to sing at a benefit for his beloved Naples,
on account of the Vesuvius disaster."

At Rudolph Spreckels' handsome house,
at Gough and Pacific Avenue,
the lawn was riven from end to end in great gashes,
the ornamental Italian rail
leading to the imposing entrance
was a battered heap.
Rudolph Spreckels, his wife, his little son,
his mother-in-law and sister-in-law and maid servants,
had set up their household on the sidewalks.

The home of John D. Spreckels,
at Pacific Avenue and La Guana Street,
is one of the finest and proudest in the city
and on it the parapet had cracked and crumbled and fallen
like so much spun sugar out of a wedding cake.
Blocks of cement had fallen from the entrancing ceiling
and at one of the upper windows
a wan, white face peered from the rich lace curtains.

Mrs. Rudolph Spreckels,
wife of the well-known financier,
presented her husband with an heir
on the lawn in front of their mansion
on Friday
when the family were awaiting
the coming of the dynamite squad
to blow up their magnificent residence.
An Irish woman, who had been called in
to play the part of midwife at a birth on Saturday,
made a pertinent comment after the wee one's eyes
were opened to the walls of its tent home.
"God sent earthquakes and babies,"
she said,
"but He might, in His mercy,
cut out sending them both together."

"I have money,"
she said,
"if I could
get it
and use it.
I have property,
if I could
realize on it.
I have friends,
if I could
get to them.
Meantime I am
going to cook
this piece of bacon
on bricks
and be happy."

Here again is an old, old woman,
with wrinkled face, paper-white,
somebody's grandmother, she is —
and she is being trundled along
in an invalid chair, her family,
with hastily made bundles
of clothes and valuables, all about her.
Great clouds of smoke
rise dull and dark on every side
and red, angry flames shoot long
tongues through them.

There is one place within pistol shot of the city
that the earthquake did not touch,
that did not lose a chimney or feel a tremor —
Alcatraz Island. Despite the fact
that the island is covered with brick buildings,
brick forts and brick chimneys,
not a brick was loosened nor a crack made.
When the scientists come to write of the disturbance
they will have their hands full
explaining why Alcatraz did not have
any physical knowledge of the event.
The scene from the island was awe-inspiring.
The crash of a falling city
filled the ears of the aroused island,
but no one understood what it was all about,
until a boat from Alcatraz landed
at the shattered wharves in San Francisco.

The old San Francisco is dead.
The gayest, lightest-hearted,
most pleasure-loving city
on this continent,
and in many ways the most interesting
and romantic,
is a horde of huddled refugees
living among ruins.
It may rebuild; it probably will;
but those who have known that peculiar city
by the Golden Gate
and have caught its flavor
of the Arabian Nights
feel that it can never be the same.
It is as though a pretty, frivolous woman
had passed through a great tragedy.
She survives, but she is sobered and different.
If it rises out of the ashes
it must be a modern city,
much like other cities
and without its old flavor.

The people of San Francisco
know the shock of calamity,
but they do not know defeat.
They will have their city again.
It cannot be the old city,
nor suggestive of the old.
Disaster seems to have swept away
the barriers that afforded pleasing
isolation. The new San Francisco
will be as other prosperous cities,
its distinctiveness only that
which springs from its site
as an outpost overlooking the Pacific.

JOHN ROBERT COLOMBO

One cannot but rejoice in the vitality of the work
and admit, not for the first time,
that Colombo is, whether a poet or an anti-poet,
one of the most brilliantly inventive
and shrewdly perceptive writers of his generation.
(Robin Skelton, *The Malahat Review*)

Author

The Mackenzie Poems
The Great Wall of China
Abracadabra
Miraculous Montages
John Toronto
Neo Poems

Editor

How Do I Love Thee
New Direction in Canadian Poetry
Rhymes and Reasons